# Index

## Childhood & Teen years



## Romantic life & Being a parent

# My Credentials

Full Name

Meaning Behind Name

Date of Birth

| Place Of Birth | Nickname/s |
|---|---|
| Height | Eye Colours |
| Hair Colours | Accent |

Any Allergies?

Attach Your Photo Here

# legacy locker

Branch of service

---

Dates of service

---

Rank

---

Military occupational specialty (MOS)

---

Units served in

---

Deployments or tours of duty

---

Awards and decorations

---

Any additional relevant information

---

# Time Capsule

## Today's Date

| President<br>Of your country | Population<br>Of Your Country |
|---|---|
| Population<br>Of Your City | Population<br>Of The World |

## The Price Of

| | |
|---|---|
| Gallon of Gas | Newspaper |
| Postage Stamp | Eggs (dozen) |
| Gallon Of MILk | Electricity (monthly bill) |
| Movie Ticket | A Cell Phone |
| Monthly<br>Mortgage payment | Mortgage<br>Interest Rate |
| Average<br>Weekly wage | Average<br>House Price |

# Early Life

## (childhood, Teen years)

# How would you describe your father?

# How would you describe your mother?

What was your preferred toy as a child?

What subject were you terrible at in school?

Who was your closest friend growing up?

Did you own any pets when you were a child?

# Can you share a funny or memorable story from your school days?

Are you still in contact with
any of your childhood friends?

Did you get any pocket money growing up?
How much was it?

# Could you tell me your most special childhood memory with your parents?

# What did your parents do for a living?

# What did your grandparents do for a living?

How was the financial situation
at home when you were a child?

Whom did you idolize growing up?

What was your favorite breakfast when you were a child?

Which was the first dish you cooked by yourself?

# What were your hobbies and interests when you were a child?

# What comes to mind when you Think about Growing up in Hometown

Were you a part of any club in high school?

Did you play any sports in high school?

What was your favorite subject in school?

How would your teachers from high school describe you?

What was your favorite hangout spot in high school?

What was your favorite band growing up?

Who was your favorite professor in high school? Why?

Have you ever admired a historical figure? If yes, why?

What do you miss the most about your college days?

Were you ever suspended from school?

# Have you ever broken someone's heart?

## What is your worst habit?

Is there anything you always
wanted to tell your parents but couldn't?

What was your first job, and how much were you paid?

What did you do with your first paycheck?

# What significant life lessons did you learn from your first job?

When did you buy your first car? How was the experience?

What was the worst job you ever had?

Is there any member of your family you wish We had met?

# The Family You Made

(Romantic life, Being a parent)

# Describe your first meeting with your spouse

# How Did You Know She is the One?

## Where did you go on your first date?

# Describe the story of your proposal.

# Where did you go for your honeymoon?

Has a romantic gesture for
your spouse ever failed badly?

# How do you and your spouse resolve conflicts?

Who is the first one to say sorry
when you and your spouse fight?

# How did you know you were ready to have children?

How many children did you want to have?

Did you plan to have children, or did it just happen?

How did you react when you learned that
you were going to have a baby?

How did you feel when you first held
your baby in your hands?

Did you face any complications when having children?

How did you change as a person after having children?

How did your relationship with your spouse
change after having children?

# Were there any disagreements between you and your partner about parenting styles for your children?

# What is the toughest thing about raising children?

# What is the Best thing about raising children?

# What was your biggest belief about raising children that turned out to be untrue?

# What do you miss the most about the time when you didn't have any children?

# What parenting advice would you give to new parents?

# Notes

# Notes

# Notes

# Service experience

# What do you remember about the day you enlisted?

49

How did you tell your family and friends
that you were joining the military?
Are there any conversations
that stand out from that time?

what were some of the reasons
that you joined the military?
How did you choose your branch of service?

# How did you imagine military life before you joined?

## What was basic training like?

# Can you describe a funny moment from boot camp?

# How did you stay in touch with family and friends back home?

# What are some things you remember most about your deployment?

Can you describe how you felt coming home from combat?

Was there anything you especially missed about civilian life?

Is there someone you served with that you remember fondly?
Can you tell me about him/her?

what are some fun things you and your friends
did together while you werw deployed?

Did you ever get caught breaking any rules?
Did you ever get away with something
you weren't supposed to do?

# When did you leave the military?
# What was that process like?

# How did your perceptions change after serving?

# How do you think your time in the military affected you?

## What did you learn about yourself?

What phrase or word was never be
the same now that you served?

# Is there anything you wish civilians understood about military service?

# What are some things you miss about being in the service?

What are some things you are glad to have left behind?

How would you have wanted to change
the conduct of the war if you could?

## Would you do it all again? Why or why not?

| Favorite Rifle | Favorite Tank |
| Favorite weapon system | Favorite piece of equipment |
| Favorite vehicle | Favorite aircraft or helicopter |
| Favorite Pistols | Favorite machine guns |
| Favorite missiles | Favorite bombers |

# Moments
# of Life

# A moment that shaped who you are today

# Positive moments of your life

# The Happiest moments in your life

# Funniest moments of your life

# Saddest moments of life

# most memorable travel experience

# Notes

# Notes

# Artistic existence

# Favourite Book

Things that like about the Book

# Favourite Movie

## Things that like about the Movie

# Favourite Song

## Things that like about the Song

# Favourite Piece of art

## Things that like about the Piece of art

# Notes

# Notes

# Regrets

Looking back on your life, are there any decisions you wish you had made differently?

Are there any missed opportunities
that you sometimes think about?

# If you could go back and give your younger self advice, what would it be?

# Are there any relationships you want to Repair?

Have you found ways to turn any regrets into positive lessons or opportunities for growth?

Is there anything you've learned from your regrets
that you'd like to share with me?

# Notes

# Notes

# Words

# of

# wisdom

How do you define success, and has your definition changed over the years?

# Is there any advice you'd like to give us?

What message would you like to share with your Family?